Planet
Earth

BIRTH OF THE DINOSAURS

MICHAEL BRIGHT

PowerKiDS press™

Published in 2018 by **The Rosen Publishing Group, Inc.**
29 East 21st Street, New York, NY 10010

Cataloging-in-Publication Data
Names: Bright, Michael.
Title: Birth of the dinosaurs / Michael Bright.
Description: New York : PowerKids Press, 2018. | Series: Planet Earth | Includes index.
Identifiers: ISBN 9781508153962 (pbk.) | ISBN 9781508153900 (library bound) | ISBN 9781508153795 (6 pack)
Subjects: LCSH: Dinosaurs--Juvenile literature.
Classification: LCC QE861.5 B69 2018 | DDC 567.9--dc23

Written by Michael Bright
Cover illustration by Mark Turner
Editor: Corinne Lucas
Designer: Alyssa Peacock

Picture credits: p 4 (t) © Stocktrek Images, Inc. / Alamy Stock Photo; p 4 (b) © gallimaufry/Shutterstock; p 5 (t) © Sisyphos23/Wikimedia; p 5 (b) © CHRISTIAN DARKIN/SCIENCE PHOTO LIBRARY; p 6 © Michael Rosskothen/Shutterstock; p 7 (t) © AuntSpray/Shutterstock; p 7 (m) © DEAGOSTINI/UIG/SCIENCE PHOTO LIBRARY; p 7 (b) © JAIME CHIRINOS/ SCIENCE PHOTO LIBRARY; p 8 (t) © Andreas Meyer/Shutterstock; p 8 (b) © Martin Shields / Alamy Stock Photo; p 9 (t) © B. O'Kane / Alamy Stock Photo; p 9 (b) © Matt9122/Shutterstock; p 10 (tl) © apple2499/Shutterstock; p 10 (tr) © Volodymyr Burdiak/Shutterstock; p 10 (b) © reptiles4all/Shutterstock; p 11 (t) © dpa picture alliance archive/Alamy Stock Photo; p 11 (b) © Catmando/Shutterstock; p 12 (t) © The Natural History Museum / Alamy Stock Photo; p 12 (b) © SanderMeertinsPhotography/Shutterstock; p 13 (t) © Discott/Wikimedia; p 13 (b) © Roger Hall/SCIENCE PHOTO LIBRARY; p 14 © Herschel Hoffmeyer/Shutterstock; p 15 (t) © Daderot/Wikimedia; p 15 (b) © MarcelClemens/Shutterstock; p 16 © B Christopher / Alamy Stock Photo; p 17 (t) © RAUL MARTIN/MSF/SCIENCE PHOTO LIBRARY; p 17 (b) © The Art Archive / Alamy Stock Photo; p 18 (t) © P.PLAILLY/E.DAYNES/SCIENCE PHOTO LIBRARY; p 18 (b) © MAURICIO ANTON/SCIENCE PHOTO LIBRARY; p 19 (t) © B Christopher / Alamy Stock Photo; p 21 (t) © Elenarts/Shutterstock; p 21 (m) © Creativemarc/ Shutterstock; p 21 (b) © NordNordWest/Wikimedia; p 22 © Cro Magnon / Alamy Stock Photo; p 23 (t) © Asia Photopress / Alamy Stock Photo; p 23 (b) © B Christopher / Alamy Stock Photo; p 24 (r) © KENNIS AND KENNIS/MSF/SCIENCE PHOTO LIBRARY; p 25 © Creativemarc/Shutterstock; p 26 © blickwinkel / Alamy Stock Photo; p 27 © Universal Images Group North America LLC / DeAgostini / Alamy Stock Photo; p 28 (t) © Valentyna Chukhlyebova/Shutterstock; p 28 (b) © Stocktrek Images, Inc. / Alamy Stock Photo; p 29 (t) © GARY HINCKS/SCIENCE PHOTO LIBRARY; p 29 (b) © Wollertz/ Shutterstock; Background images and other graphic elements courtesy of Shutterstock.com.

Manufactured in China

CPSIA Compliance Information: Batch #BS17PK: For Further Information contact Rosen Publishing, New York, New York at 1-800-237-9932.

contents

the
SURVIVORS

251 million years ago (mya) during the Triassic **period**, planet Earth was recovering from the most devastating **mass extinction** of all time — the Permian-Triassic extinction. Millions of plant and animal **species** had disappeared, but not everything was wiped out. Large reptilian **predators** and their **prey** somehow survived — and no one knows how!

the burrower

The surviving reptiles included the earliest dinosaurs. They lived alongside other animals that looked like dinosaurs but were from other reptile groups. One of these was *Lystrosaurus*, meaning "shovel lizard." It was about the size of a pig, a plant eater and had a horny beak with two large **tusk**-like teeth. It probably dug a nesting burrow, which could have been a safe refuge when things got tough outside.

Long tail for balance.

up and running

Another survivor was the meat-eating *Euparkeria*. It was about 24 inches (60 cm) long and **nocturnal**. Its back legs were quite long, so scientists believe that it could rise up and run for short distances on its two back legs, a feature it shared with the meat-eating dinosaurs that followed.

Sea Survivors

In the sea, **marine** reptiles called placodonts were also among the survivors. The early ones were similar in shape to marine iguanas, but bigger. They were up to 6.5 feet (2 m) long and big enough to beat sharks in a fight. Later species had more ferocious predators to scare off, like the 10-foot (3m) *Ceresiosaurus*. It had a long neck, large flippers, and was a fast swimmer. For protection, the placodonts developed bony plates on their back, and some looked just like sea turtles.

Placodus fed underwater like a marine iguana.

HERE WE GO AGAIN

About 200 mya, when the planet had settled down after the Permian–Triassic extinction, life was wiped out again, this time by severe global warming. Scientists think this Triassic–Jurassic extinction killed off most competitors of the early dinosaurs, but the dinosaurs survived. This allowed them to dominate the planet for the next 135 million years.

GEOLOGICAL TIME

Scientists divide the 4.6 billion years since Earth formed up to the present day into geological **eons**, **eras**, periods, **epochs**, and ages. The dinosaurs lived during the Mesozoic era. Figures are in millions of years, except for the Holocene.

Eon	Era	Period	Epoch
Phanerozoic (541 to present)	Cenozoic (65.5 to present)	Quaternary (2.588 to present)	Holocene (11,700 years to present) Pleistocene 2.58 mya to 11,700 years)
		Neogene (23.03 to 2.58)	Pliocene (5.333 to 2.58) Miocene (23.03 to 5.333)
		Paleogene (66 to 23.03)	Oligocene (33.9 to 23.03) Eocene (56 to 33.9) Paleocene (66 to 56)
	Mesozoic (251 to 65.5)	Cretaceous (145 to 66)	
		Jurassic (201.3 to 145)	
		Triassic (252.17 to 201.3)	

the first
DINOSAURS

The first dinosaurs lived in the Triassic period. Their name means "terrible lizard." They were a varied group of reptiles, but they all had one thing in common — their legs were directly beneath their body, unlike lizards and crocodiles whose legs are splayed out to the sides.

earliest known dinosaur

Nyasasaurus was one of the first dinosaurs. It lived about 245 mya. From nose to tail, it was 10 feet (3 m) long, although its torso was no bigger than a dog. It could walk on its long back legs. Like many of the early dinosaurs, it ate plants and small animals.

in the shadows

Eoraptor was a predator that lived about 230 mya. It was about 3 feet (1 m) long and ran on its two long back legs, so it was a good **sprinter**. Its diet was mixed, and it tore food apart with its sharp teeth and the claws on its hands. *Eoraptor* lived alongside more powerful predators, such as *Saurosuchus*, a 23-feet (7 m) crocodile-like reptile, so it had to use its speed to get out of trouble.

Sharp claws for tearing food.

Strong arms for grabbing and holding prey.

Powerful hind legs for running fast.

FIRST MAMMALS

Some people think that mammals **evolved** after the dinosaurs had gone, but they actually developed alongside them. Scientists have found species that show the change from reptile to mammal appeared about 200 mya. The creatures were generally small, about 5 inches (12 cm) long, and shrew-shaped, like *Megazostrodon*. This animal was probably nocturnal and ate insects and small lizards.

jungle carnivore

Herrerasaurus was up to 20 feet (6 m) long and an example of the large dinosaurs to come. It could move swiftly on its back legs and follow prey through jungles. Its "hands" had elongated fingers with long claws on two of them. Its jaws had a flexible joint that could slide backwards and forwards, and were lined with large saw-like teeth. This meant the predator could slice through meat. *Herrerasaurus* was a **forerunner** of the theropod dinosaurs, the group that would eventually evolve to include *Tyrannosaurus rex*.

the MEAT EATERS

During the Jurassic and Cretaceous periods, between 201–66 mya, predatory dinosaurs ruled the Earth. These dinosaurs, known as theropods, ran on long and powerful back legs and were armed with strong jaws and claws. Most were meat-eating predators known as **carnivores**.

lizard hunter

Not all of the top predators were big dinosaurs. *Compsognathus* was no bigger than a turkey but it had small, sharp teeth that could grasp small lizards and insects between them. It lived on small coastal islands, during the late Jurassic period, and despite its size, it was probably the top predator on the coastal islands.

Long, slender tail.

terrible claw

A speedy predator during the Cretaceous period was *Deinonychus*. It was about 11 feet (3.4 m) long and had jaws lined with 70 curved, blade-like teeth. It might have hunted in packs and attacked its prey by jumping onto its back and lashing out with large, curved claws — just like how some birds of prey hunt.

Short but powerful arms with two-clawed fingers.

tyrant lizard king

One of the largest meat eaters was the infamous *Tyrannosaurus rex*. It was up to 40 feet (12.3 m) long and walked at 25 miles per hour (40 kph) on its back legs. It had a huge head with a large brain and very powerful jaws. It had the strongest bite of any known animal.

SPEEDY DINOS

Apart from their long tails, the ostrich dinosaurs resembled modern-day ostriches and could run just as fast. One of the fastest was *Struthiomimus*. It could reach 28–50 mph (45–80 kph) over short distances — faster than a racehorse. Unlike most of their theropod relatives, ostrich dinosaurs had no teeth. They were probably **omnivores**, which means they ate plants and animals. Their speed also kept them in front when they were chased by larger theropods, such as the tyrannosaur *Gorgosaurus*.

MONSTER
predators

Tyrannosaurus rex, or *T. rex* for short, might be the most famous, but it was not the only giant predatory dinosaur roaming the Earth during the Jurassic and Cretaceous periods. Its relatives were even bigger …

Its slender skull was about 5 ft (1.6 m) long.

monster packs

Giganotosaurus was longer than a *T. rex* — about 46 feet (14 m) long — but less bulky, with a more slender skull. It may have hunted in small packs to bring down giant plant-eating dinosaurs, such as *Andesaurus.* Its jaws and teeth would have made slicing wounds. It could run at about 25 miles per hour (40 kph) and as a fierce predator, it was at the top of its food chain towards the end of the Cretaceous period.

shark-like teeth

Each tooth was 8 in (20 cm) long.

One dinosaur who was a similar size to *Giganotosaurus* was *Carcharodontosaurus*. It was about 46 feet (14 m) long and weighed up to 16.5 tons (15 metric tons), more than the weight of two large African elephants — the heaviest land animal alive today. Its enormous jaws were lined with **serrated** teeth, similar to those of the great white shark.

monsters fishing

Two enormous dinosaurs have been identified as fish-eaters — *Baryonyx* and *Spinosaurus*. *Baryonyx* had a very large claw on one finger and long, narrow, crocodile-like jaws. It was up to 33 feet (10 m) long, but it was small next to the fish-eating *Spinosaurus*, the largest predatory dinosaur that ever lived. *Spinosaurus* was up to 49 feet (15 m) long and had spines on its back that probably supported a sail-like structure. It may have behaved like a modern grizzly bear, scooping up salmon from river **estuaries**.

Sometimes walked on four feet.

COPE'S RULE

In the 19th century, American scientist Edward Drinker Cope suggested that, if climate and food supply are stable, the body size of animals increases as they evolve. During the Jurassic and Cretaceous periods, dinosaurs seemed to be doing just that — they got bigger and bigger. In 2015, Cope's theory was proved correct by looking at the height of humans. People were 5 inches (13 cm) taller in the 1970s than in the 1870s.

FEATHERED
dinosaurs

Many of the meat-eating theropod dinosaurs had feathers, like birds. The feathers could have been to keep the animal warm or for show, like a bird of paradise's feathers. They also allowed the smaller dinosaurs to glide or even fly through the air, but the larger animals couldn't fly.

early flyer

Tail feathers also helped *Epidexipteryx* to balance on branches.

Microraptor was one of the world's smallest dinosaurs. It was about the size of a crow with a long tail. It had two pairs of feathered wings on its arms and legs. The wings were capable of gliding, but might also have given the animal true flight. Its feathers were probably black, glossy, and **iridescent**, like those of a modern starling. It fed on small creatures in trees, and occasionally on lake fish, and lived during the Cretaceous period.

PRESERVING COLORS

Color is not preserved well in fossils, but color-producing sacs, called melanosomes, have been found in the fossilized feathers of *Sinosauropteryx* and several other small theropods. Scientists have worked out that this small, ground-hugging dinosaur might have had bristle-like feathers with light and dark stripes along its tail, like a modern ring-tailed lemur.

warm dinosaur

The largest predatory dinosaur known to have had feathers was *Yutyrannus*, meaning "feathered tyrant." It was 30 feet (9 m) long and its thread-like feathers were up to 8 inches (20 cm) long. They covered its whole body, with the longest feathers around its shoulders. It lived in an area with cold winters, which was unusual for the Cretaceous period. The average annual temperature was only 50°F (10°C) and the feathers probably kept it warm. *Yutyrannus* was a relative of *T. rex*, so the tyrannosaurs might also have had feathers on parts of their body, especially when they were young and more vulnerable to the cold.

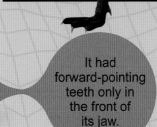

It had forward-pointing teeth only in the front of its jaw.

visual display

Epidexipteryx had the earliest known example of **ornamental** feathers. It had four long tail feathers, which must have been to impress potential mates, like the display of a peacock. This dinosaur was about 18 inches (45 cm) long, including its tail feathers, and lived during the Jurassic period.

GIANT
plant eaters

During the Triassic period, the plant-eating dinosaurs known as prosauropods grew to be very large. But then the sauropods came along, who were also plant-eaters, during the Jurassic and Cretaceous periods. They grew to immense sizes, becoming the largest land animals to have ever lived. The biggest of them all were the enormous titanosaurs.

bit of a stretch

Plateosaurus was a prosauropod that lived during the late Triassic period. It was one of the first dinosaurs to grow to more than 26 feet (8 m) long. If it stood on its hind legs, it could reach up into the trees with its long neck. A curved claw on its thumb pulled branches towards its mouth, and could also have been used in self-defense.

Brachiosaurus had a very long, giraffe-like neck.

giant giraffe-neck dinosaur

One of the heaviest Jurassic sauropods was *Brachiosaurus*. The 85-foot (26 m) animal had a huge body and a long neck, with front legs longer than its back legs. It could stretch up 30 feet (9 m) to the tops of trees with little effort, like a giraffe.

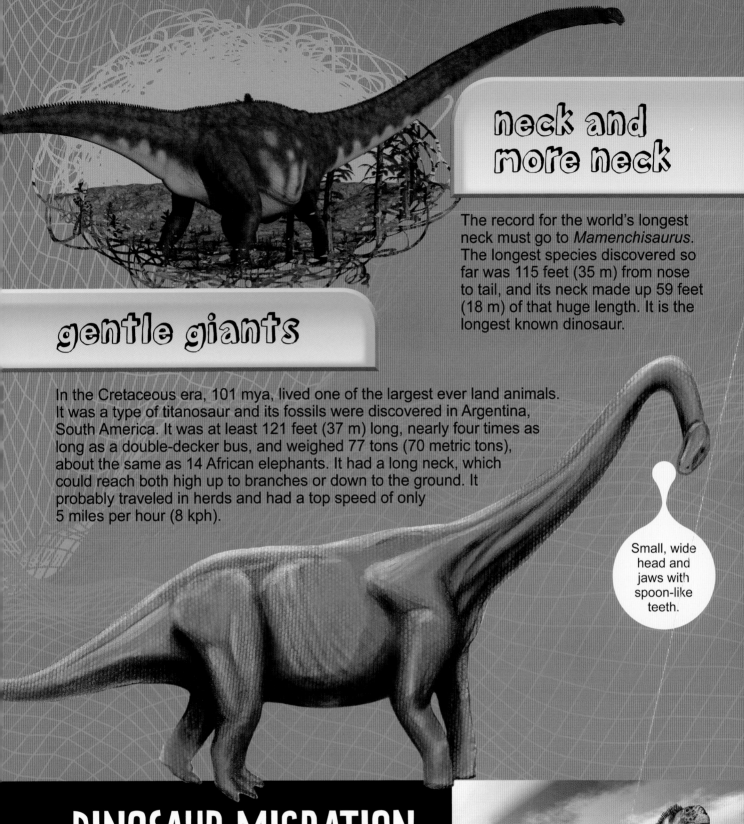

neck and more neck

The record for the world's longest neck must go to *Mamenchisaurus*. The longest species discovered so far was 115 feet (35 m) from nose to tail, and its neck made up 59 feet (18 m) of that huge length. It is the longest known dinosaur.

gentle giants

In the Cretaceous era, 101 mya, lived one of the largest ever land animals. It was a type of titanosaur and its fossils were discovered in Argentina, South America. It was at least 121 feet (37 m) long, nearly four times as long as a double-decker bus, and weighed 77 tons (70 metric tons), about the same as 14 African elephants. It had a long neck, which could reach both high up to branches or down to the ground. It probably traveled in herds and had a top speed of only 5 miles per hour (8 kph).

Small, wide head and jaws with spoon-like teeth.

DINOSAUR MIGRATION

Like many birds and animals, dinosaurs migrated. The huge *Camarasaurus* went on lengthy journeys as the seasons changed. They avoided summer **droughts** in lowland areas by moving to higher ground, where it was cooler, wetter, and there was plenty to eat. They returned to the lowlands during the wet winter season.

DUCKBILLS

The plant-eating hadrosaurs, or duck-billed dinosaurs, are named for their duck-like faces. They lived during the Cretaceous period. Many had wide beaks and jaws lined with hundreds of tiny teeth for munching tough plant material. Several had bizarre horn-shaped crests on their head. Most species traveled in big herds.

Small, solid crest on top of its head.

honker hadrosaur

Edmontosaurus was a crestless duckbill, but it might have had an area of loose skin on the top of its snout that could inflate to make a bellowing call, like an elephant seal. It was a large animal, up to 43 feet (13 m) long.

Chambers in the crest amplified sounds.

helmet lizard

Corythosaurus had a large, crest-like half plate on its head. The crest was about 28 inches (70 cm) tall, and similar to that of the modern cassowary bird.

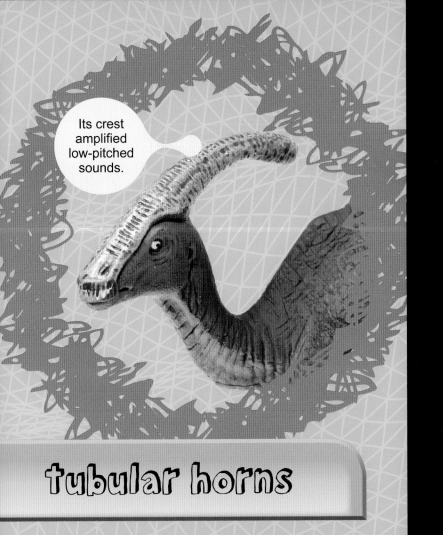

Its crest amplified low-pitched sounds.

tubular horns

Parasaurolophus had a curved, hollow, horn-like crest on top of its head. Inside, breathing tubes ran from the back of its throat to the top of its horn and back to its nostrils, so this dinosaur could play its crest like a trumpet. It meant it could communicate to others of its own kind.

GOOD MOTHERS

Duck-billed dinosaurs traveled together in large herds, and nested together. Scientists have found nesting **colonies** of *Maiasaura*, which means "good mother lizard." These duckbills dug nests in the ground, where they laid up to 20 eggs. They fed their hatchlings shoots and leaves until they were about 3 feet (1 m) long and able to follow the herd.

The nests of other types of dinosaurs have also been found. Some titanosaurs, for example, laid their eggs in a large circle. Others placed their eggs in straight lines. And the fossil skeleton of the theropod *Oviraptor* has been found lying over a clutch of eggs as if she was brooding them like a mother hen.

CRASH HELMETS and SPIKES

Several types of plant-eating dinosaurs would fight predators who tried to eat them, rather than run away. To help strike fear into their attackers, they had nasty weapons to attack with, such as sharp spikes, and strong defenses to protect their head and neck, such as horns and bony shields.

three horns

The most famous horned dinosaur is *Triceratops*, a type of ceratopsian dinosaur that looked like a modern rhinoceros. It had a bony shield around its neck and three long, sharp horns on its head. It probably used them to challenge rival *Triceratops* or to confront large predators such as *T. rex*.

Horns on the snout and above the eyes.

Large bony neck frill.

Protoceratops

Regaliceratops

Styracosaurus

decorative shields

The shields and horns found on different ceratopsians vary a lot between species. The sheep-sized *Protoceratops* had a neck shield but no horns, while *Regaliceratops* had a shield with frills that looked like a crown. *Styracosaurus* had a neck shield edged with enormous spikes. Some of the larger head shields broke easily and had large holes in them, so it is thought they were more for display to **intimidate** a rival than for fighting.

body slamming

Pachycephalosaurus was one of the boneheads. It had a thick roof to its skull with bony projections, like a crazy crash helmet. It is thought that the male animals slammed their heads into the sides of rivals, like male giraffes do today. These combats were the way they decided who was top dino.

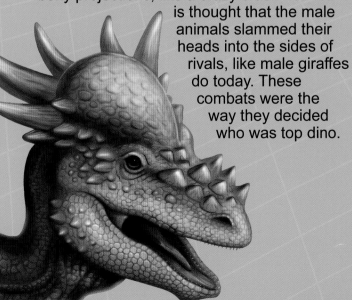

DINOSAUR DUNG

The ceratopsians were plant eaters, but the boneheads ate both plants and animals. Scientists know what dinosaurs ate because they find either stomach contents inside fossil skeletons or they examine fossilized dung. Pieces of dinosaur dung are called coprolites, and they range in size from 1/2 an inch (12 mm) to more than 24 inches (60 cm). One of the largest was from a tyrannosaur found in Canada. It contained the fossilized remains of a bonehead, which must have been its last meal.

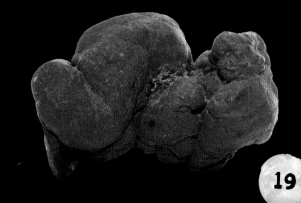

ARMORED
dinosaurs

Plant-eating dinosaurs had to protect themselves from predators and they did it in different ways. The stegosaurs had armored plates and spines on their back and tail, and lived in the latter part of the Jurassic period, while the ankylosaurs had body armor and spines along their sides, and lived in the Cretaceous period.

plum-brain dinosaur

Stegosaurus can be recognized by the two rows of broad, vertical plates along its back. The plates were quite delicate and are thought not to have been for more than defense. They were probably involved in controlling body temperature or were a visual display. The animal was up to 9 m (30 feet) long, but it had a brain the size of a plum, so it could not have been very bright.

tough armor

Sauropelta lived at the same time and in the same place as *Deinonychus* (see page 8), but it could fend off the predator's slashing attacks with a tough, armored back and fearsome spines around its neck.

Thick triangular spines behind the head

Edmontonia was 20 feet (6 m) long, weighed 3 tons (3.3 metric tons) and was built like a tank. It had an armor-plated head and massive body armor with bony plates and huge forward-pointing spines. It shared its living space with a type of tyrannosaur, named *Albertosaurus*, but all it needed to do was to plow straight into the predator to scare it off.

Muscular tail with heavy club.

wrecking ball

A type of ankylosaur known as *Euoplocephalus* had a low-slung, heavily armored body, but with the added defense of a heavy club on the end of its tail. *Euoplocephalus* could have stopped an attack from a large predator by swinging its tail club against the predator's legs and breaking them. It could have also squared up to a rival *Euoplocephalus* and exchanged alarmingly violent blows.

MEDICAL RECORDS

From looking at fossils, scientists think that dinosaurs were a healthy bunch. Some show bone **fractures** to the head, backbone, or ribs, probably from fights between males at mating time. Infections were few but a duck-billed dinosaur was found with a dental **abscess**. With all the teeth packed into its jaw (see page 16) it must have hurt!

undersea HUNTERS

While some dinosaurs went fishing, they did not go into the open ocean, but some of their reptilian relatives did. They were the ichthyosaurs, plesiosaurs, pliosaurs, and mosasaurs. They were not dinosaurs, but the top marine predators of their day, and some were real monsters.

streamlined

Ichthyosaurs lived in the Triassic period and became extinct before the end of the Cretaceous period. They had a similar torpedo shape to modern dolphins and some species were huge, up to 52 feet (16 m) long, whereas others were small at just 3.3 feet (1 m). They all had flippers and big eyes, so they could hunt in the deep sea, and some species had a dorsal fin. Ichthyosaurs also had rows of **conical** teeth for catching fish and squid.

Dorsal fin stops the animal from rolling over.

GIANT SHELLFISH

The ammonites were relatives of modern nautiluses, and they dominated the open oceans at this time. They were also a readily available food source for some of the giant marine reptiles. The largest fossil found so far was *Parapuzosia*, which lived about 78 mya. It was 8.5 feet (2.6 m) across. Now, that would have been a mouthful even for a monstrous reptile!

sneaky hunters

Another impressive group of reptiles were the plesiosaurs. They were recognizable by their long neck, small head, short tail, paddle-like flippers and broad, short body. Some were up to 49 feet (15 m) long; others were only 5 feet (1.5 m). They were slow-moving hunters that caught small marine creatures. Their small head and long neck meant they could sneak up on prey without disturbing the water so their prey didn't notice them getting closer.

Elasmosaurus had an extremely long neck, even for a plesiosaur.

apex predators

Pliosaurs were similar to plesiosaurs, but most had short necks. They were up to 56 feet (17 m) long, and fast-swimming hunters. They were the top marine predators during the Jurassic period, making them **apex** predators and literally the terror of the seas. But another creature later became the scariest sea predator — the lizard-like mosasaurs, who were alive towards the end of the Cretaceous period.

Kronosaurus had jaws lined with sharp, conical teeth.

FLYING
reptiles

Throughout history, different animals have taken to the air and been able to fly. Insects, birds, and mammals flew and still do — and at one time, so did reptiles! The reptile flyers were the pterosaurs, and they lived at the same time as the dinosaurs.

Stork-like bill.

giant of the skies

The largest animal ever to have flown was a pterosaur called *Quetzalcoatlus*. It had a **wingspan** of up to 40 feet (12 m), nearly four times that of the wandering albatross, which has the longest wingspan of any bird alive today. It had a long neck, and a long, pointed, toothless beak, and a crest on the top of its head. It is thought to have fed much like a modern stork, stabbing at small animals in the grass or in streams. It also walked on its four limbs when on the ground.

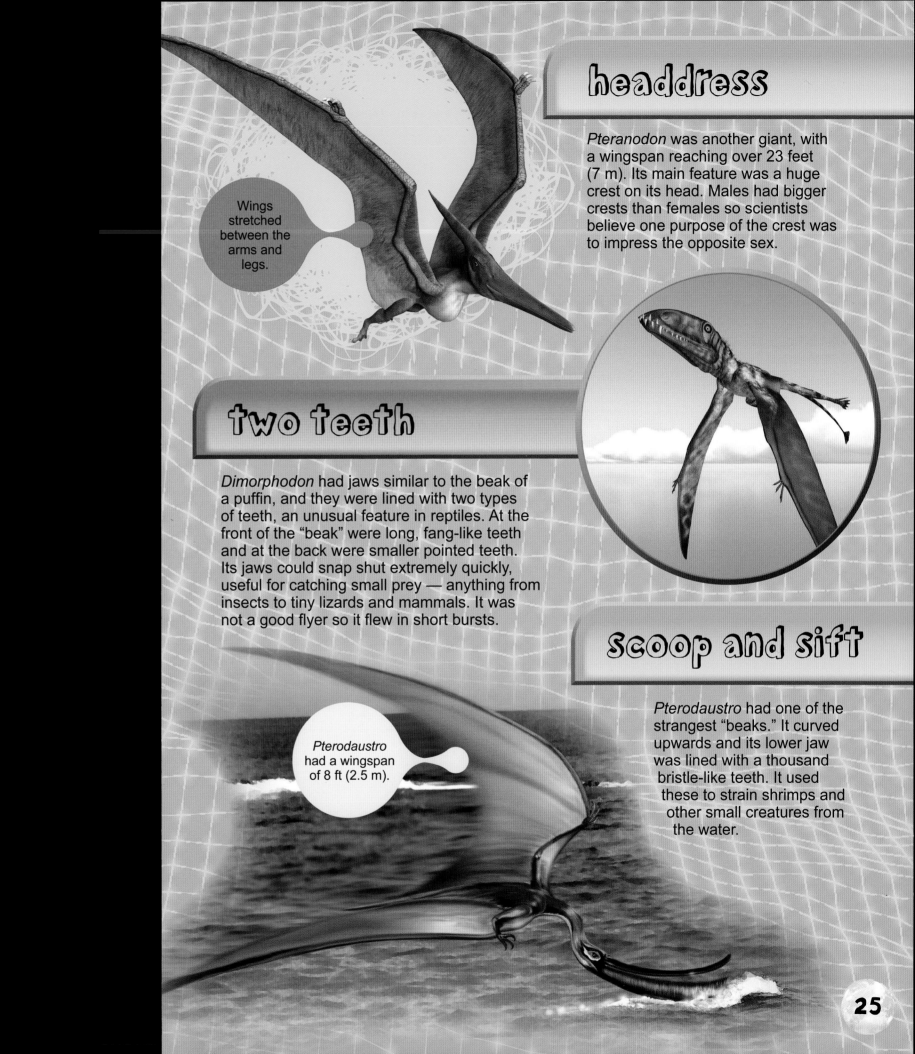

headdress

Pteranodon was another giant, with a wingspan reaching over 23 feet (7 m). Its main feature was a huge crest on its head. Males had bigger crests than females so scientists believe one purpose of the crest was to impress the opposite sex.

Wings stretched between the arms and legs.

two teeth

Dimorphodon had jaws similar to the beak of a puffin, and they were lined with two types of teeth, an unusual feature in reptiles. At the front of the "beak" were long, fang-like teeth and at the back were smaller pointed teeth. Its jaws could snap shut extremely quickly, useful for catching small prey — anything from insects to tiny lizards and mammals. It was not a good flyer so it flew in short bursts.

scoop and sift

Pterodaustro had a wingspan of 8 ft (2.5 m).

Pterodaustro had one of the strangest "beaks." It curved upwards and its lower jaw was lined with a thousand bristle-like teeth. It used these to strain shrimps and other small creatures from the water.

demise of the
DINOSAURS

All good things must come to an end, and 65 mya, the time of the dinosaurs and their relatives came to a close. The precise cause of this remains unclear, but scientists have several ideas about what might have happened to the dinosaurs.

volcanoes

A series of massive volcanic eruptions might have been the cause of the dinosaurs' death. The volcanoes created vast **lava fields**, known as the Deccan Traps, across the land that now makes up India. The eruptions started about 66 mya, and lasted for 30,000 years, just before the disappearance of the dinosaurs. The volcanoes would have given off huge amounts of **noxious** gases into the atmosphere, and volcanic dust would have blocked out the Sun, causing a global climate change that saw a drop in temperature of 35.6° F (2° C).

Impact crater.

asteroid

At about the same time as the volcanic eruptions, an **asteroid**, about 6.2 miles (10 km) across, slammed into the Earth where Mexico's Yucatan Peninsula is today. The impact threw up huge amounts of dust and debris that blotted out the Sun for at least a year, and immediately after the blast a great fireball of burning gases caused wildfires right across the planet. Plant life would have been burned or later died because of the lack of sunlight. This event is known as an "impact winter." With few plants surviving, the plant-eating dinosaurs died out, and then their predators did too.

mass extinction

The dinosaurs were not the only casualties of the volcanoes and asteroids. The giant marine reptiles and flying reptiles also disappeared, along with the ammonites in the sea. In all, it is thought that three-quarters of all species of plants and animals on Earth became extinct.

lucky break

With only 25% of all animals and plants left alive, there were new opportunities. For example, some species took over the places once ruled by dinosaurs. However, not all of the dinosaurs died out … birds are living dinosaurs!

birth of
THE BIRDS

Bird-like reptiles began to appear during the Jurassic period, but the first true birds did not arrive until the Cretaceous period, about 100 mya — 45 million years before the dinosaurs became extinct.

rise of the birds

Birds evolved from feathered, meat-eating theropod dinosaurs. Their features appeared one by one during the Mesozoic era (251–66 mya). At first they ran on two legs, then they had simple feathers, and then a wishbone, followed by more complex quill-like feathers. Finally they developed fully working wings, which meant they could fly.

Longest flight feathers are in the middle of the wing.

dinosaurs in color

One of the earliest bird-like dinosaurs was *Anchiornis*, which lived about 160 mya, in the Jurassic period. It had down-like body feathers, and flight feathers on its arms and long legs, giving it double wings. Scientists have been able to work out its color — its body feathers were gray and black, the top of its head was reddish-brown, and the wing feathers were white with black tips. Feathers on its lower leg were gray and those on the foot were black.

small is smart

While all the other dinosaurs were getting bigger and bigger, the **ancestors** of the birds became smaller. Being small was key to their survival. It meant they could move around in the trees and take advantage of new feeding opportunities that larger animals couldn't. Because they were small, birds could more easily evolve from gliding to powered flight. However, identifying the animal that was the "first bird" is almost impossible, but there are a couple of fossil animals that must have been close.

Archaeopteryx had feather "pants."

early bird

The first bird-like fossil to be discovered was *Archaeopteryx*. It lived about 145 mya. It had feathers and wings but probably could not fly like birds do today. It also had similar features to early reptiles, such as teeth and a long, bony tail. It might not have been a direct ancestor of birds, but maybe closely related. However, since its first discovery in the 1860s, scientists have argued constantly about whether it actually was the first bird … and that argument continues to this day.

glossary

abscess painful collection of pus in the body

ancestor animal from which later animals evolved

apex top or peak

asteroid large space rock

carnivore animal that eats only meat

colony group of living things that live together

conical shaped like a cone

drought a long period without rain

eon largest division of geological time

epoch smallest division of geological time

era geological time that is shorter than an eon and longer than a period

estuaries the wide part of a river that meets the sea

evolve develop gradually

fracture crack or break

intimidate fill with fear

iridescent shiny and showing colors

lava field area of hot liquid volcanic rock that has cooled and become solid

marine something that lives in the sea

mass extinction disappearance of many plants and animals at the same time

nocturnal active at night

noxious unpleasant and harmful

omnivore animal that eats both plants and animals

ornamental decorative

period geological time that is shorter than an era and longer than an epoch

predator animal that hunts and eats other animals

prey animal that is eaten by another animal

serrated jagged like a saw blade

species a type of plant or animal

sprinter one who runs fast over short distances

tusk greatly enlarged tooth

wingspan distance between one outstretched wing tip and the other

Books

Dangerous Dinosaurs (2011)
Tom Jackson
Gareth Stevens Publishing

Jurassic World Dinosaur Field Guide (2015)
Dr. Thomas R. Holtz Jr. and Dr. Michael Brett-Surman
Random House Books for Young Readers

Killer Dinosaurs (2016)
Liz Miles
Gareth Stevens Publishing

National Geographic Kids Ultimate Dinopedia: The Most Complete Dinosaur Reference Ever (2010)
Don Lessem
National Geographic Children's Books

The Complete Illustrated Encyclopedia of Dinosaurs & Prehistoric Creatures (2014)
Dougal Dixon
Southwater

Websites

PowerKids Press has developed an online list of websites related to the subject of this book. This site is updated regularly. Please use this link to access the list:
www.powerkidslinks.com/pe/dinos

index